The kingdom of Arendelle stood by a deep lake. It was a very happy place. At night, the Northern Lights created beautiful patterns in the sky.

But the king and queen were worried.

Their eldest daughter, Elsa, had magical powers. She could freeze things and create snow, even in summer!

Their youngest daughter, Anna, loved her big sister. The two girls had fun playing together in the snow and ice.

One night, Elsa accidentally hit Anna with her powers.

The king and queen rushed the girls to see the magic trolls, hoping they could help.

The trolls said that Anna would get better, but that Elsa's powers would get stronger. She had to learn how to use them carefully.

Back at Arendelle, Elsa found it difficult to control her powers. She decided to keep away from Anna, to keep her little sister safe.

The trolls changed Anna's memories. She couldn't remember a thing about Elsa's magic. Instead, she believed that Elsa wanted nothing to do with her.

The two sisters grew older. By the time Elsa became queen, they hardly knew each other.

Anna felt lonely for a long time, so she was very happy when she met a handsome prince called Hans.

Anna and Prince Hans liked each other straight away.
Hans asked Anna to marry him and she agreed. But Elsa was angry. "You don't know him well enough. You can't marry him," she said.

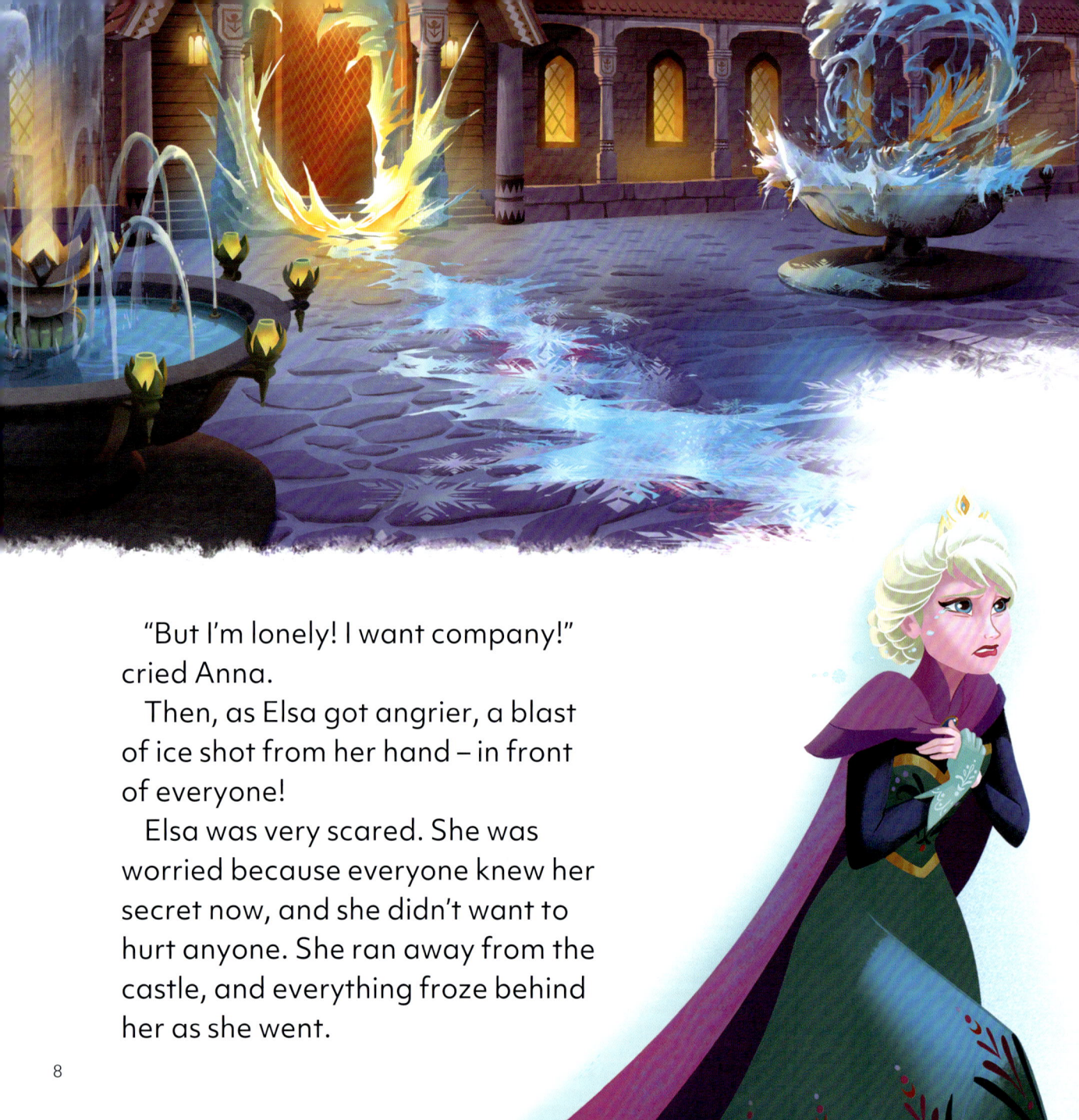

"But I'm lonely! I want company!" cried Anna.

Then, as Elsa got angrier, a blast of ice shot from her hand – in front of everyone!

Elsa was very scared. She was worried because everyone knew her secret now, and she didn't want to hurt anyone. She ran away from the castle, and everything froze behind her as she went.

Elsa climbed up to the mountains. She felt better there. She was on her own and could use her powers properly for the first time. She created patterns of snow and ice, and even an ice palace!

She was happy at last.

Anna went to look for Elsa. She knew about her sister's secret at last, and she wanted them to be together again.
  Anna climbed to the mountains. But she fell off her horse into the snow.
  She went to look for help in a nearby shop.

In the shop, Anna met a young man. He was frozen from head to toe! The young man was angry. His job was collecting ice, and a snowstorm in the middle of summer was bad for his business.

But he knew where the storm was coming from. He could take Anna to Elsa.

The young man was called Kristoff. Anna paid him to take her up to the North Mountain to find Elsa. His reindeer, Sven, went with them.

As they reached the top of the mountain, Anna, Kristoff and Sven looked at the beautiful view. Elsa had thrown a blanket of sparkling ice over everything.

Elsa had also created a snowman, and the snowman was alive!

The snowman was called Olaf. He was very happy that Anna was going to try to bring back summer. He liked the idea of warm weather. Olaf offered to take them to Elsa.

As they walked, they saw the amazing ice palace that Elsa had created using her magical powers.

Anna admired the ice tower and Elsa's magical powers. But she really wanted Elsa to come home.

Elsa was worried that the people of Arendelle were angry with her, and that she would hurt them with her magic.

The two sisters argued. Elsa didn't want to hurt Anna, but she hit her with a blast of ice.

Then, Elsa created another snowman called Marshmallow. He was much bigger than Olaf.

The big snowman scared Anna, Kristoff, Sven and Olaf, and they left the mountain in a hurry!

After they escaped, Kristoff realised that Anna's hair was turning white. Kristoff took her to see the trolls. He hoped that they could help Anna like they had before.

The trolls said that Elsa had frozen Anna's heart. Before long, she would be completely frozen. "Only true love can melt her icy heart," said the trolls.

Olaf and Kristoff rushed Anna home to Arendelle. They wanted Hans to give her a kiss of true love.

Back in Arendelle, Prince Hans had been helping everyone during the storm. Then Anna's horse arrived back in Arendelle – without Anna!

Hans took a group of people out to look for Anna … but they found Elsa first. The men were mean to Elsa. They thought she was dangerous. They took her back to Arendelle and put her in prison.

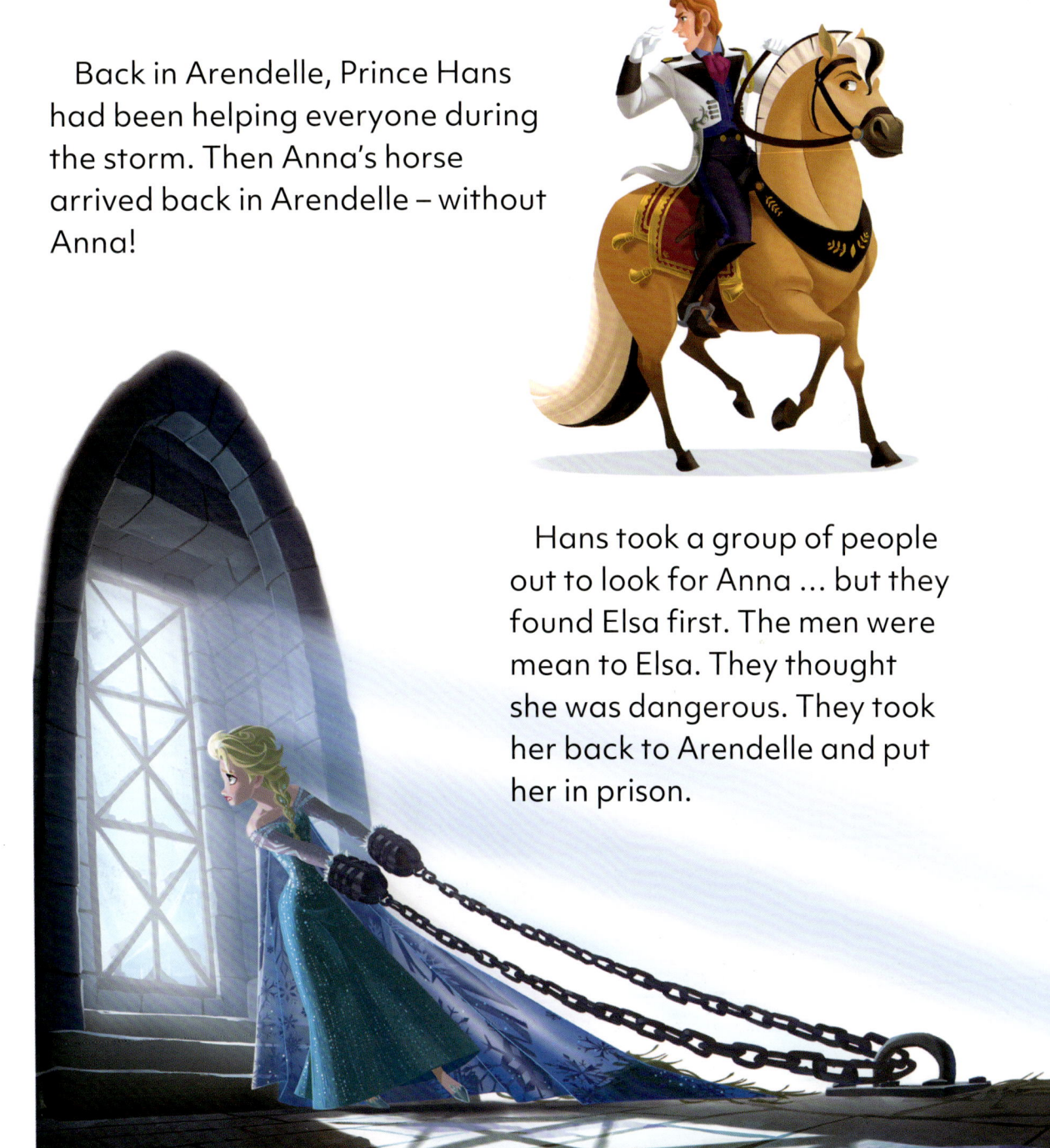

Kristoff took Anna back to Arendelle. But Hans didn't want to kiss her. He didn't love her. He only wanted to marry Anna so that he could rule Arendelle. Anna was very upset. But Olaf knew that Kristoff was in love with Anna. Kristoff's kiss could save her. As Anna walked towards Kristoff, she saw that Elsa was in danger …

Anna threw herself in front of Elsa, stopping Hans' sword from hitting her sister. But Anna turned into a block of ice.

Elsa threw her arms around Anna and cried. She didn't want to lose her sister. Suddenly, Anna began to melt. Elsa had shown true love towards her sister and the spell had been broken!

With Anna's love, Elsa brought back summer.

The two sisters promised to love each other forever. The people of Arendelle gave Elsa a warm welcome when she came home.

Kristoff decided to stay in Arendelle, and Olaf too … with the help of Elsa's magical powers.

They were all together and happy at last.